Practical Solutions for Busy Lives

(simple celebrations)

BARBOUR
PUBLISHING

© 2004 by Barbour Publishing, Inc.

Written by Vicki J. Kuyper with Snapdragon Editorial Group, Inc.

ISBN 1-59310-210-0

All Scripture quotations in this publication are from **THE MESSAGE**. Copyright © by Eugene H. Peterson 1993, 1994, 1995. Used by permission of NavPress Publishing Group.

Illustrations © Mary Lynn Blasutta.

Published by Barbour Publishing, Inc., P.O. Box 719, Uhrichsville, Ohio 44683
www.barbourbooks.com

Our mission is to publish and distribute inspirational products offering exceptional value and biblical encouragement to the masses.

Member of the
Evangelical Christian
Publishers Association

Printed in China.
5 4 3 2 1

Contents

Section 3: *Just for the Fun of It*

Introduction

Remember when you were a little girl and your mom was in charge of all the family birthdays, holiday celebrations, and special occasions? You may have been told to set the table or wrap a few gifts, but basically you just sat back and waited for the big day to arrive. The memories of those meaningful events will last a lifetime.

Trouble is, you are "the mom" now. You look at the family and friends clamoring around you with their questions and lists, and it suddenly becomes clear—it's all up to you!

This handy little *Moms on the Move* book was written in recognition of the huge task you face as you strive to keep the "special" in those special times you prepare for those you love. We've filled it with creative ideas, packed with the simple instructions you will need to carry them out, and even included a dose of inspiration for an often-needed boost to the spirit. Our hope is that *Simple Celebrations* will be the ideal mom guide to carry you beyond the planning and restore the childhood wonder of it all.

Baby Shower Blessings

Every child begins the world again....
—Henry David Thoreau

Just as a shower of rain provides the earth with the moisture it needs to grow a healthy crop, a baby shower is given to help provide a mom-to-be with what she'll need to begin the all-important task of raising a child. But moms need more than cribs, diapers, bath toys, and car seats. They need the support of other women.

Traditional showers tend to focus on cute decorations, elaborate refreshments, and the chance to "ooh" and "ahh" over baby gifts. You can simplify your job as hostess, as well as magnify the shower's impact, by filling a mom's heart, in addition to her nursery.

Before the gifts are opened, have each guest share a piece of advice, a Scripture verse, a handy parenting tip, or a prayer for the unborn child. Encourage your guest of honor to share what she's looking forward to most about being a mom, as well as what she's most hesitant about. Keep the conversation positive and upbeat. Celebrate not only the miracle of birth but the true privilege of motherhood.

Setting Up the Celebration:

- Send out invitations at least three weeks in advance.

- Prepare simple finger food, such as veggies and dip, fruit kabobs, tea cookies, cheese and crackers, and lemonade.

- Purchase and wrap a small door prize, such as a bottle of bubble bath, candle, decorative soap, or potpourri.

- Provide a comfortable chair for the guest of honor. Decorate it with ribbons, and perhaps even a "Mom-to-Be" sign, to keep other guests from occupying it. Place a trash bag nearby for discarded gift wrap.

- Place a small "gift" table near the chair, with your own shower gift on it.

- Make a name tag for each guest. Prepare a few extra blank tags, in case guests arrive who have not RSVP'd. If you're feeling creative, fold small triangles of construction paper into a diaper shape and fasten with tiny safety pins. Inside one name tag, put a squirt of mustard. Whoever gets this name tag wins a door prize! (You can also put a sticker under one chair to signal who wins the door prize.)

- If young children are going to be attending the shower, arrange for a baby-sitter who will help them play their own "shower" games in another part of the house.

Instructions:

- As your guests arrive, show them where to place their gifts, give them their name tags, then invite them to help themselves to some food and to take a seat.

- Give your guests about twenty minutes to chat, then get the festivities rolling by announcing the door prize.

- Invite your guests to share a word of wisdom, etc., for the new mom. Don't put anyone on the spot by going around the room. Let your guests share if and when they feel comfortable.

- As your guest of honor opens her gifts, make a list of names and gifts to help the mom-to-be with thank-you notes later.

- Enjoy the time together!

Make It Memorable

You and your guests can encourage the mom-to-be long after the shower is over with the gift of your words. Include a brightly colored three-by-five-inch index card with each invitation. Ask each guest to use one side of the card to write a prayer, Scripture verse, or piece of advice for the new mom. When your guests RSVP, remind them to bring their cards to the shower. After everyone has shared their cards aloud at the shower, give the cards to the new mom, so she can keep them in her baby book to support and encourage her in the days, and years, to come.

simp**le** another Celebration

SPECIAL OCCASIONS

Long-Distance Wedding Shower

May your love knot be sealed with heaven's wax!
—Irish Blessing

Weddings are typically not simple celebrations. They often tax the time, energy, and financial resources of everyone involved—including that person who takes on the responsibility of hosting a shower.

Purchasing both a shower gift and a wedding gift can be expensive for those close to the bride and groom. Also, the addresses of those on the guest list can be scattered all over the country. A nice alternative to sending costly gifts through the mail is organizing a long-distance recipe shower. It's easy on the budget, only takes about an hour or two of your time, and provides the newlyweds with a unique keepsake. Chances are, they'll put this shower gift to use much more frequently than the crystal goblets and silver serving pieces they're bound to receive on their wedding day.

Word to the Wise: It isn't the cost of a gift that makes it valuable. It's the care with which it's given.

Items Needed:

- The names and addresses of friends of the bride and groom

- Double-sized recipe cards

- Self-addressed envelopes

- Copies of a brief letter asking the guests to write their favorite recipe on one side of the card and return it, with a current photo, in the enclosed envelope by a designated date.

- An inexpensive, self-adhesive photo album.

Kids Can Too!

You can add a little humor, and a lot of memories, to a recipe shower by including children's "recipes" in the album. Invite your own children, as well as the children of those who are already submitting a recipe, to write out instructions on how to prepare their favorite dish—from memory. If the children are too young to write, parents can write out the instructions and let the kids illustrate the page.

Encourage kids to describe the ingredients they think would go into their favorite food and what Mom has to do to make it. Example: "S'mores—make sure Mom says it's okay. Melt a marshmallow in your fireplace. Don't let it catch on fire. Put the gooey marshmallow on a cracker with a piece of candy bar on it. Wash your hands before touching the furniture."

11

Instructions:

- Once recipe cards have been returned to you, place one recipe and its corresponding photo on each page.
- If desired, make a title page at the beginning of the book. Use your wedding invitation as a decorative accent, if you like.
- Mail or deliver the "shower" to the bride and groom.

Even if the bride and groom live nearby, a recipe shower is a great alternative to a traditional celebration for coworkers, neighbors, or church groups. When that first anniversary rolls around, you may even want to send along a second batch of recipes organized on additional self-adhesive photo pages that can be easily added to the book.

another simple celebration

Wedding Anniversary Memory Makers

"Do you remember when..." bonds people together for more than shared chromosomes. Stories are thicker than blood.

—Daniel Taylor

While big, extravagant gifts may be fun to give and receive, they are not the ingredient that makes an anniversary memorable. It's the relationship itself that's being celebrated. Make your special day even more special by first considering your own love story. What makes it unique? How did you meet? What first attracted you to each other? What is your favorite wedding day memory? What's the funniest thing that has ever happened to you as a couple? What dreams do you share for the future?

Use your memories as touchstones to help create a festive home atmosphere. Tell your children stories about how you fell in love. Bring out your wedding photos. Read them an old love letter. Help your children help you plan a romantic retreat that will celebrate the two of you.

Being a wife is just as important as being a parent.

Idea Starters

- Write things you love about your husband on individual construction paper hearts. Place them where he'll find them—the front seat of his car, the bathroom mirror, his pillow, pinned to his bath towel, etc.

- Shower your husband with anniversary cards, one for each year of marriage. (You don't need to purchase cards. Simple note cards or even folded index cards will do. It's what you write inside that counts!) Place one in his shoe or under his razor, so he'll find it as he's getting dressed in the morning. Hide the rest in other places he'll be visiting throughout the day.

- Encourage your children to write down what "being married" means. Then, read what they've written at dinner.

- Play a CD of songs that were popular while you were dating, while you're eating dinner or driving to a restaurant.

- If you have dinner reservations, drop off a framed photo of the two of you from your dating days (as geeky as possible!) at the restaurant earlier in the day. Ask that it be set up at your table for when you arrive. It makes a great touchstone for reminiscing and encourages extra attentiveness from the restaurant staff.

- Let your children help you make a small cake. Decorate it with your original wedding cake topper or a single rose. Feed it to each other (no forks allowed!) after dinner.

- Make a sign that reads "Honeymoon Suite" and put it on the door of your bedroom. Let your children help you come up with the ideas on how to make the room especially romantic.

Approach your spouse with the same loving intent that you do your children. Take an honest interest in his day. Celebrate his successes. Support him through his failures. Pray for him. Praise him in front of others. Ask him about his dreams—then, help him pursue them. Take time just for the two of you, every week—no matter what. Kiss him good night and thank God for him in the morning.

Allow your kids to see a marriage relationship being celebrated and enjoyed. What you and your husband model at home can have a great impact on your children's future relationships—not to mention your own level of joy and loving commitment.

MOM Meditations

As you watch your children grow, the milestones in their lives seem to pass by so quickly—first steps, first words, first day at school. Their needs are so immediate, and constant, that motherhood can easily take center stage, pushing your equally important role of "wife" to the sidelines. But, as your kids grow and mature, so do you and your husband. Continuing to grow in the same direction, instead of apart, during this hectic time takes both commitment and creativity.

simple another Celebration

15

Birthday Parties for Children

The moment after Christmas every child thinks of his birthday.

—Stephen Uys

In a child's world, the two biggest days of the year are Christmas and his or her own birthday. When it comes to birthdays, parents too often try to make the day memorable by spending a lot of money on gifts and entertainment. Fortunately, options are available.

Do your kids and yourself a favor: When it comes to birthdays, keep it simple. Don't stress your budget, or your emotions, by planning a party that begs to be featured on *Lifestyles of the Rich and Famous*. Honor your kids with your attention, the company of their best friends, one gift they'd really enjoy, and lots of little surprises throughout the day.

Surprise your child by putting candles in her pancakes at breakfast. Take the day off work and "kidnap" your child to a movie matinee. Surprise your child at school by joining him in the cafeteria for lunch. The possibilities are as endless as your imagination.

Word to the Wise: Surprises that are treasured in the heart last longer than those held in the hands.

Setting Up the Celebration:

- Try and clear your own schedule as much as possible for your child's birthday.
- Carefully consider your child's age and personality when making plans. Ask yourself questions, such as, "Does my child like interacting with lots of people or just a few close friends? Is my child old enough to handle winning and losing games, or should I stick to gift bags for guests with non-competitive activities?"
- Call any guests you'd like to invite as soon as you have a firm date and time. This is usually more time efficient than sending children invitations. Give the parents of the guests a quick call a few days before the party to reconfirm their child's attendance.

- Arrange for a surprise guest. Have an adult friend dress up as your child's favorite super-hero or cartoon character. Take digital photos of each child with the surprise guest. E-mail the photos, along with a thank-you note, a few days later.
- Instead of a traditional birthday cake, surprise your child by serving "Cupcake Cones." Place flat-bottomed ice cream cones in muffin-tin cups on a baking sheet. Prepare boxed cake batter according to the instructions. Fill each cone halfway with cake batter. Bake according to the directions on the package for cupcakes. Cool 15 minutes. Frost and decorate as desired.
- Put a surprise note on your child's pillow to be discovered at bedtime. Tell your child what a wonderful surprise God gave you the day your child was born.

17

Writing thank-you notes is more than just a common courtesy. It's a way of encouraging your children to have more thankful hearts. After the Big Day, don't let more than a week go by before helping your child express his or her thanks to their guests.

If your children are too young to write, ask them to draw a picture of themselves playing with the gift or let them dictate a brief thank-you note for you to write out. Help your kids understand that a gift isn't wholly theirs until they've expressed their thanks to the person who gave it.

Cost Savers

With the variety of gift bags, boxes, decorative paper, ribbons, and bows available, deciding how to wrap a gift can be as much of a challenge as deciding what gift to buy.

When it comes to wrapping, think outside the box! Use small white plastic trash bags or plastic grocery sacks turned inside out. Tie the gift closed with a simple piece of ribbon, a twist tie from a loaf of bread, a pair of fun shoelaces, or a balloon tied to a piece of string. If the gift is for a young girl, use a ponytail band, a hair ribbon, or a barrette to close the bag. Fabric remnants, foil, and lunch bags also make great last-minute gift wrap. Or, make the "wrap" part of the gift. Use a new laundry bag, purse, sand pail, lunchbox, or a backpack as the "gift wrap" for smaller, inexpensive trinkets.

You can also let your kids make their own wrapping paper for friends' gifts by decorating newspaper with stickers or butcher paper with their own artwork. (Caution: When wrapping any gift for a child under the age of four, you should not use plastic bags or small items they may be tempted to put into their mouth.)

another simple celebration

Wild Things

Cupcakes? Check. Nonstaining lemonade in cups with lids and straws for kids? Check. Large, fully caffeinated beverage close at hand for me? Check. Goodie bags for guests? Check. Other mothers' cell numbers in case of emergency? Check.

"Let the chaos begin!" Lauren whispered quietly to herself as the doorbell rang, announcing the first little guest.

Ryan was turning five today. Intuitively, Lauren knew that the days of simply inviting the relatives over for cake were behind them. For the last ten days, Ryan's entire vocabulary seemed to revolve around the words "my birthday," which was immediately followed with an emphatic "PARTY!"

Lauren had never been much of a "party" person. She liked to commemorate her special day with hikes in the woods, quiet picnics with her family, or even a mocha latte and a good book. Why God had given her a son who was in love with loud motorcycles, frenzied video games, and anything that involved running, shouting, and occasionally breaking things was a mystery to her. *Maybe that's the point,* she thought. Maybe Ryan will help unlock the mysterious appeal of all the "wild things."

Just then, Lauren's mom came racing in from the backyard, a golden autumn leaf stuck randomly in her hair. "I told the boys they could jump in the piles of leaves," she told Lauren breathlessly. "I hope you don't mind."

Yet another "wild thing," Lauren thought, glancing at her mom. In Lauren's mind, "Nana" and Ryan were kindred spirits. At times, Lauren felt like an outsider, someone who just followed Ryan and Nana around, cleaning up their messes. "I'm sure Dennis and I can rake them together again later," Lauren said with a sigh. "Mom, we only have an hour and a half before the boys' mothers come back. Why don't we let the boys expend some of that energy on the piñata?"

"Great idea!" Nana said enthusiastically, heading for the closet to retrieve the motorcycle-shaped piñata. "I'll go hang it up on the swing set. You get Ryan's bat." The door slammed as Nana hurried off toward the giggling boys buried in fallen leaves.

By the time Lauren made it outside, her mother had already taken down the swings, hung the piñata, lined up the boys, and was tying a bandana over the eyes of the first lucky guest to get a swing at the cardboard motorcycle. Each of the six boys swung wildly, nearly hitting the other boys in line, but thoroughly missing the piñata that hung above their heads. When Ryan's turn arrived, Nana helped point him in the right direction, adding her own strength to his wild swing. With a mighty *whack* the motorcycle finally broke in two and—nothing but shreds of black and white paper fell to the ground.

"Didn't you fill it with candy?" Nana whispered to Lauren frantically.

"I didn't know I had to!" Lauren said in a panic, feeling dangerously close to tears.

As Ryan took off his blindfold, Nana disappeared into the house. She returned with her arms filled with Halloween candy from the pantry, which she threw madly into the air, whooping and hollering as though this was exactly what was supposed to happen once a piñata broke.

The boys jumped and dove with delight, searching through the leaves for sweet treasure. Nana joined them, her heart obviously filled with as much childish delight. For a moment, Lauren hesitated, watching the brawl erupt into wild giggles.

"This is the best party ever!" Ryan said to no one in particular. Then he smiled at his mom and pulled on her leg. "C'mon!" he pleaded.

Lauren smiled as she let herself fall into the pile of leaves and treats. She came up laughing, with leaves in her hair and a chocolate bar in her fist. Maybe wild things can be wonderful after all. . . .

the end

Teen Tunes Birthday Party

Instant availability without continuous presence is probably the best role a mother can play.
—Lotte Bailyn

Most teens and even some preteens feel that the best birthday parties have minimal adult supervision with maximum musical volume. But, that doesn't mean you should step back from being involved in celebrating your teen's special day. The longing to be celebrated is just as strong in a teen as it is in a toddler.

Get your teen involved in the planning of his or her own party. As "Mom," you set the rules, such as budget, number of people who can be invited, and the time the festivities need to end. But let your teen have ample say in what the party is going to be like. Instead of playing "chaperone," play the role of photographer and snack delivery woman. There are plenty of ways to participate in the party while giving teens their own space.

Setting Up the Celebration:

- Have your teen ask guests to bring a few of their favorite CDs.
- Decorate the room for the party with crepe paper and posters of your son's or daughter's favorite musical groups. (The posters can be given away as prizes, if your teen wants to include games.)
- Order pizza or grill burgers. (Remember, when it comes to teens, quantity, instead of quality, is usually a prerequisite for party fare.)
- Set out bowls of snacks, such as chips, cookies, nuts, or candy.
- Have trash bags accessible to encourage "picking up" during the party, instead of waiting until afterward.
- Have a CD player or karaoke machine readily available in the party area.

- Have guests take turns playing DJ. Give each guest a slot of time or three-song limit, so everyone who wants to gets a turn.
- Have the pizza or burgers available about an hour after the party starts.
- Use a music poster for a take-off on "Pin the tail on the donkey." Give every guest a small piece of paper with adhesive on the edge. Have guests draw an original "tattoo" on the paper. Blindfold the guests one at a time and have them stick the tattoo on the rock star. Give prizes, such as the poster, for the most creative, most artistic, most interesting place for a tattoo, etc.
- Set a time when the music goes off and a video everyone would enjoy watching together goes on. This helps quiet a party down as the hour gets late. Have plenty of popcorn ready, in case they want to watch a second feature!

Clean-up after a teen party can be a big job if the topic hasn't been addressed with your teen before the party starts. Five minutes before the party ends, have your teen ask everyone to spend a few minutes throwing out trash, making sure everyone has their own CDs, and putting any furniture that's been moved back into place. Make sure it's understood that anything that isn't picked up that night automatically becomes a chore your teen will have to do the next day.

simple *another* *Celebration*

Good IDEA

You don't have to wait for your teen's birthday to invite friends over for a party. The more you open your home to your teen's friends, the more you'll get to know and enjoy them. Work at making your home one that welcomes teens. Build a library of teen-friendly DVDs. Prepare a few extra servings when you're cooking dinner, so your kids will feel free to invite friends to join your family for meals. (Any leftovers will also serve as easy to reheat after-school snacks for famished teens and their friends!) While the teen years are expensive, try not to cut corners in the food department. Keeping the fridge and pantry well stocked with snacks will help make your house the place to be!

Turn Back Time
Adult Birthday Party

*If you carry your childhood with you,
you never become older.*
—Abraham Sutzkever

The farther away people get from the year they were born, the less likely they seem to want to celebrate it. But life—and the people who add so much love to it—are always worth celebrating, no matter how high or low their chronological age.

Celebrate the significant life of the one whose birthday you're honoring by starting at the beginning—the year of his or her birth. A lot has happened since then! Use that as the focus of your party—what's changed, what's remained the same, even what dreams the guest of honor has yet to fulfill.

You can make the party as simple or as elaborate as you like. You could decorate the room with old photos, trophies, and yearbooks belonging to the guest of honor. You could have a CD playing music that was popular during that era. Just keep your focus on the unique life of the one having the birthday. It will make this trip down memory lane a smooth and enjoyable ride for both the guests and the guest of honor.

24

Word to the Wise: You are a unique gift of God—one worth celebrating year after year.

Setting Up the Celebration:

- Check an encyclopedia "yearbook" out of the library to see what was happening during the chosen "birth year" in terms of history, inventions, entertainment, clothing styles, and fads. If desired, you can make up a short trivia guessing game from what you learn.
- Ask each guest to bring along a baby picture, with an address label attached to the back so it can easily be returned. Tell them not to show it to anyone else.
- Ask guests to come dressed appropriately for the birth year of the party. For example, bobby socks, poodle skirts, and leather jackets for the fifties or tie-dyed shirts, ponchos, and love beads for the sixties. Encourage creativity, not expense. Thrift stores are a great resource for "authentic" costumes.
- With whatever food you choose to serve, include a theme snack appropriate to the times. If fondue was the latest craze—make fondue. Or offer a Spam buffet or serve your snacks in clean "TV dinner" trays.

- Collect photos from guests at the door.
- Relax and enjoy each others' costumes while munching on "theme" snacks.
- Give each guest a pre-printed guest list. Set out the baby pictures. Have each guest match a name with a photo. Present a photo frame to the guest who guesses the most correctly.
- If desired, have a "birth year" trivia contest and hand out prizes for the best costumes.
- Open gifts.
- As the evening winds down, put in a "vintage" video and enjoy.

Reminiscing is an important part of any birthday party. While the baby photos and costumes will be a natural conversation starter, it's also fun to spend a few minutes talking about when and how guests first met the person celebrating the birthday.

Kids Can Too!

Children can still be made to feel that they are an important part of a birthday celebration even when they are not invited to the actual party. Have your kids help you set a buffet table, blow up balloons, fold napkins into simple shapes. They can also help out by preparing easy appetizers, such as spreading cream cheese or peanut butter on precut pieces of celery, sticking grapes and squares of cheese onto frilly-ended toothpicks, or putting a small dab of smoky cheese spread on halved pecans.

simple *another celebration*

"Hurray for You!" Congratulations Party

Lord, turn the routines of work into celebrations of love.
—John Oxenham

Whether it's graduating from high school, receiving a promotion at work, earning a spot on the first-grade T-ball team, or losing five pounds, life is filled with reasons to offer heartfelt congratulations. Some accomplishments may merit more fanfare than others, but a simple family "party" at the dinner table is no less important than an all-out bash that takes weeks of preparation.

If just the word "party" makes you feel a bit squeamish, take heart. You can sincerely celebrate the victory of someone you love—in a meaningful and memorable way—even during the craziest seasons of life. If you keep a few simple items on hand at home (see the next page for a specific list), you won't even have to fit an extra trip to the store into your busy day.

The most important ingredient for this kind of celebration—an attentive involvement in the lives of those you love—won't cost a thing. Know what your spouse and kids are striving to achieve, and struggling to overcome. Celebrating victories, both big and small, is one practical way that your family can support one another.

Word to the Wise: A true victory is when you do your best, regardless of whether you come in first or last.

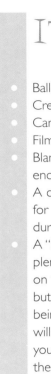

Items Needed:

- Balloons
- Crepe paper streamers
- Candles
- Film in your camera
- Blank note cards, for words of encouragement
- A crown or other fun party hat for the guest of honor to wear during the meal
- A "Hurray for You" plate. There are plenty of "You Are Special" plates on the market you can purchase, but anything that sets apart the one being honored at the dinner table will do. Use one place setting of your good china and tie balloons on the chair or ribbons on one setting of silverware.

Instructions:

- Put a "We're so proud of you" note in a lunchbox, on a family member's pillow, taped to a bedroom door, or at the dinner table.
- Decorate the guest of honor's place at the table.
- If possible, prepare the guest of honor's favorite meal for dinner.
- Put candles in the main course or dessert to add a festive air.
- As a family, sing, "We're so very proud of you! We're so very proud of you! We're so proud of you (name). We're so very proud of you!" to the tune of "Happy Birthday" before beginning dinner.
- Take a photo of the guest of honor. (Keep a "Hurray for You" photo album on hand with self-adhesive pages. Be sure to label each photo with the date and reason for the celebration.)

Remember, you don't want the sincerity of a "Hurray for You" party to wear off by doing the same thing too frequently. Sometimes a simple note saying "I'm proud of you, because—" is the best celebration of all.

simple another Celebration

MOM Meditations

Teaching your children what truly deserves honor in this world is an important task. So is helping them understand the part God plays in both the victories—and defeats—they face. Celebrating your children's efforts, along with their accomplishments, will help them better understand these truths. Practicing perseverance, self-sacrifice, the courage to take risks, unconditional love, humility, honesty, and diligence when there are no rewards other than knowing that what you're doing is pleasing to God are all occasions worthy of congratulations.

Help your kids understand that God throws "Hurray for You" parties for those He loves all the time! Join in His celebration by thanking God for what He is doing in and through your children's lives, as well as your own.

29

Going-Away Open House

The best moments of a visit are those that again and again postpone its close.
—Jean Paul Richter

A "Going-Away Party" seems like an oxymoron. Imagine celebrating something that makes you feel sad! The truth is that what you're celebrating is the fact that out of a whole wide world filled with people, God allowed your path to cross with that of someone you grew to love. What a gift!

The greater the gift, the harder it is to say good-bye, especially for kids. Having a party is a positive way to help everyone ease into this time of transition—those who are moving, as well as those who will remain behind.

Because a going-away party has the potential to be tough emotionally, simplicity is more important than ever. Forget the games, decorations, and formal invitations. Set out some simple prepackaged snacks and open your house for a few hours, allowing friends the opportunity to simply drop by and offer their best wishes.

Word to the Wise: Even though you may be miles apart, those you love are always close at heart.

Setting Up the Celebration:

- Work closely with those who are leaving to set the time, date, and duration of the open house. If possible, schedule the open house between mealtimes.

- Ask your guests of honor for a list of friends they'd like to invite.

- Contact guests by phone or E-mail, as soon as the date is set.

- Keep your refreshments simple. Serve one beverage, such as lemonade, and set a few bowls of snack foods (e.g., veggies and dip, pretzels, mixed nuts, wrapped candy) around the main room.

- Have index cards with the guests of honor's new address, phone number, and E-mail address on them for guests to take home with them.

- Purchase an inexpensive address book. Set it by the front door and encourage guests to fill in their own personal information. Give the address book to your guests of honor as a going-away gift.

Good IDEA

Dealing with the heartache of having a friend move away is usually one of the first encounters your child will have with loss. You can help your child cope in a positive way by doing a few simple things—praying with your child that God will help the friend feel at home in the new place, e-mailing photos, marking the friend's new hometown on a map. Help your child understand that love has nothing to do with location. They can still love someone whom they can't see. Use this lesson to help them better understand how they can love God, even though they can't see Him.

Simple Going-Away Gift Ideas

Since packing is usually well under way when a party is scheduled, refrain from giving the guests of honor anything that is large or breakable. Greatly appreciated are:

- Prepaid phone cards

- Stamps and stationery

- Return address labels preprinted with your friends' new address

- A small photo album or picture frame with a favorite photo from a moment you've shared together

- A book highlighting sights and activities near your friends' destination

Whether those who are going away are making a permanent move or fulfilling a temporary assignment, the most important thing a party can do is reassure those leaving that they will not be "out of sight, out of mind." When the party is over, make sure your commitment to your friend is not. A simple phone call, E-mail, or "Welcome to your new home" note can be a great encouragement in the first weeks after a move. Taking a few moments out of your busy schedule to let your friends know that you're thinking of them can keep you close at heart, even when time and miles separate you.

simple another celebration

SIMPLE HOLIDAY CELEBRATIONS

SIMPLE HOLIDAY CELEBRATIONS

New Year's Eve, Family Style

Ring out the old; ring in the new.
—Alfred, Lord Tennyson

New Year's Eve is the perfect night to overlook your kids' regular bedtime schedule and join together for a sleepy-eyed family celebration. Prepare the food together as a family earlier in the day. Then, relax and snack while you watch movies, play board games, or put together a family-sized jigsaw puzzle. Make sure that the only attire allowed after seven o'clock is pajamas!

When midnight arrives, awaken any of those who may have inadvertently fallen asleep, grab your noisemakers and blankets, and head out onto the front or back porch for a few minutes of rowdy fun. Your kids will enjoy the fact that this is the one day out of the year when staying up late and making lots of noise is encouraged.

The recipes and activities you choose to include in your celebration will depend on the ages and interests of your children. Whatever you choose, this late-night jubilee is bound to become a highly anticipated family tradition year after year.

Family-Friendly Recipes

Homemade Eggnog—1 egg, 2 tbsp. sugar, a dash of salt, 1 c. milk, and ½ tsp. vanilla per serving. Break eggs into a bowl and beat until thick and smooth. Add sugar and salt, beating until they have dissolved. Beat in milk and vanilla. Serve hot or cold.

Funky Drumsticks—1 lb. ground beef, 12 soda crackers, 1 tsp. salt, 1 egg, and 6 wooden skewers to serve 6. Set oven at 450°. Put ground beef, salt, and egg in bowl. Mix thoroughly. Divide into 6 parts. Put crackers in a bag and crush with a rolling pin. Place crumbs on waxed paper. Shape meat around skewers like drumsticks. Roll in crumbs. Place in greased baking pan, baking for 30 minutes, turning once.

Snowman Cake—Make two round one-layer cakes, according to directions on the package. Cover a large piece of heavy cardboard with foil. Place cakes next to each other on covered cardboard. Frost with white icing. Let the kids "decorate" the snowman themselves. Snacks such as dried fruit, chocolate chips, cinnamon candies, coconut, pretzels, licorice, shelled nuts, and sprinkles can be used.

Family-Friendly Activities

- Have an indoor "snowball" fight using large marshmallows. Cleaning up should include the whole family.

- Purchase an oversized calendar for the new year. Together, fill in important dates, such as birthdays, anniversaries, and the first and last day of school.

- Create a New Year's Memory Book. Using a loose-leaf notebook, record each member of the family's favorite memory from the year gone by. Add the names of best friends, favorite teachers, movies, and songs, as well as any memorable family events.

Record the height of each child and his or her "resolution" for the new year. Take a family photo at midnight to add to your keepsake. Read the previous year's entries together every New Year's Eve.

- Try to keep the morning of New Year's Day open so that the whole family can sleep in. Though family traditions for New Year's Day are as unique as the families who plan them, try to keep the day simple. Bagels and fresh fruit for breakfast and a Crock-Pot of soup for lunch is a low-stress way to start the New Year. You may even want to make a family tradition of having Chinese food or pizza delivered for the evening meal.

simple another Celebration

Make It Memorable

When you celebrate New Year's Eve as a family, it's the perfect time to make a "family" resolution.

The key is to agree on one goal as a family, then keep each other accountable to make sure the resolution is kept. Choose a resolution that strengthens your family as a whole. Allow every member of the family to share ideas about what the resolution should be.

Write your resolution in your New Year's Memory Book, but also on another piece of paper or poster board. Post it somewhere that the whole family can be reminded of the promise you've made each other. Then, when the next New Year's Eve rolls around, discuss how keeping last year's resolution made an impact on your family.

Valentine Dinner for Two

When one is in love, a cliff becomes a meadow.
—Ethiopian Proverb

How a day dedicated to honoring several Christian martyrs named Valentine became associated with love, greeting cards, and chocolate is a bit of a mystery. But, regardless of the history behind today's traditional cupids and candy hearts, Valentine's Day is the perfect chance for a busy mom to schedule a special "date" with the most important man in her life.

With restaurants and baby-sitters often overbooked, a Valentine's dinner at home can be an easy, and economical, way to enjoy a memorable evening. All you need is a little planning and creativity to inspire a lot of romance.

The first thing you need to do is forget about eating at the kitchen table. Tonight is all about sweet surprises. Have a picnic in front of the fireplace, in the backyard, or even in your bedroom. Take time to talk, nibble an appetizer—or an ear—and just enjoy the fact that God has brought you two together to learn firsthand what love is all about.

Word to the Wise: Love is much more than an emotion. It's a sacrificial gift of yourself where you put another's needs before your own.

Setting Up the Celebration:

- Choose a "secret" location for your Valentine rendezvous. Make a treasure map, write clues, or leave a trail of candy hearts that will lead your spouse to the picnic.

- Set a blanket or tablecloth on the floor of your "secret spot." Illuminate the area with candles.

- Set out a buffet of simple hors d'oeuvres.

- Set his Valentine card out with the buffet.

- Play a CD of instrumental music softly in the background.

- Turn off all cell phones.

- Be waiting at the secret spot— in your nightgown, if you like.

Suggestions for your Valentine Buffet:

- A variety of cheeses, deli meats, pâté, and crackers. (You can purchase heart-shaped crackers from specialty food stores.)

- Grapes

- Veggies and dip

- Salsa or hot artichoke dip with chips

- Heart-shaped cookies

- Fancy chocolates

Time for private, intimate conversation with your spouse is often at a premium for busy moms. Take advantage of this special evening by thinking of a few topics you'd like to bring up over dinner. Stay away from anything that has to do with finances, repairs that need to be made, or problems you've been wanting to discuss. Concentrate on getting to know your husband better. No matter how long you've been married, there's always more to learn. Ask "what if" kinds of questions like, "If you could have three wishes, what would they be?"

simple another Celebration

Good IDEA

When planning time for "just the two of you," one of the main questions on every busy mom's mind is "What do we do with the kids?" If your children are small, you can plan a late dinner for the two of you after their bedtime. If your children are old enough to occupy themselves for awhile, rent a special video and set up a Valentine's picnic for them in front of the TV. You can even include your children in part of your own celebration by inviting them to play the part of "waiters," serving individual courses of the picnic to you and your husband.

You can also set up a baby-sitting swap with a friend. Have one mom watch all of the kids while the other mom enjoys a picnic with her spouse.

39

Paper Hearts

Cathy glanced through the stacks of faded greeting cards, questionable crayon renderings, and graduation announcements that filled one of numerous cardboard boxes surrounding her on the attic floor. *How can I possibly throw any of this away?* Cathy asked herself.

As she began to reseal the box, leaving its contents fully intact, the corner of a red construction paper heart caught her eye. As she pulled its softly frayed edges from the midst of her other paper treasures, Cathy couldn't help but smile. The words "Now and Forever" were still as vivid as they had been more than twenty years earlier on that very first Valentine's Day. That was the year she'd met Mark.

"You can't really celebrate Valentine's Day until you have a real live Valentine," she'd always told her friends. And that year, for the first time, she did. For days,

40

Cathy cut out construction paper hearts. On each one, she wrote one of the many reasons why Mark had captured her heart. "Because you make me laugh. . . Because you listen well. . . Because you love God even more than you do me. . ." There had been seventy-two hearts in all, not because there were only seventy-two reasons for loving Mark, but because she'd run out of paper.

While Mark was at class that day, Cathy posted one heart on the door of his dorm room that read, "I love you for so many reasons!" Inside, she carefully taped the remaining hearts all over his room. On his bed, Cathy placed a heart-shaped chocolate chip cookie with the final paper heart set on top of it—"Now and Forever." Then, she went back to her room.

When the awaited knock came at her own door, Cathy was confused by the expression on Mark's face. Instead of gratitude, there was a look of absolute horror. "I'm sorry!" Mark said, his voice shaking with emotion. "I totally forgot it was Valentine's Day! I didn't get you anything!"

For a moment, Cathy could feel disappointment begin to well up in her heart. Here it was, her first real Valentine's Day, and her Valentine had forgotten all about her. *That's not true,* Cathy argued with her own emotions. *He didn't forget about me; he just forgot about Valentine's Day. There's a difference.*

"I promise I'll never forget again," Mark said, with a tender, repentant kiss.

And he hadn't. Through three more semesters of college, those tough first years of marriage, two sets of diapers, and two high school graduations, Mark had never forgotten Valentine's Day—or to let Cathy know how much he loved her.

The last twenty-five years were a crazy quilt of laughter, longing, tears, breakthroughs, and breakdowns. Ordinary days were interwoven with adventure. Tough times were balanced out by good old-fashioned commitment—and unexpected joy. But, the thread that ran through it all was love.

Cathy put the heart carefully back into the box and sealed it up tight. Memories like that were worth hanging onto—now and forever.

the end

"What I Love About You" Valentine Party for Kids

We are all born for love; it is the principle of existence and its only end.

—Benjamin Disraeli

Valentine's Day is the perfect time to invite your kids and their friends to join together for a time of fun and laughter while at the same time giving them a lesson in love. If your children are attending school, they probably will have had plenty of Valentine treats during the day. What that means for you is that they are already in a party mood—and that one simple snack is all you need to provide!

This party works as well with just a few friends or with all the kids on the block. Once again, since the children may have already had a busy day, keep the party short and simple—an hour and a half is plenty of time to make a long-lasting memory.

Word to the Wise: God doesn't just love us—He is love. Describe what real love is like and you describe the essence of God's unchanging character.

Items Needed:

- One lunch sack for each guest
- Stickers, crayons, and markers
- Red construction paper hearts or inexpensive valentines (enough for each child to give one to every guest, as well as to themselves)
- One bowl for each guest
- White boxed cake mix, batter prepared
- Nondairy whipped topping
- Cupcake holders and muffin tins
- Marbles
- Food coloring
- Nonstaining beverage

Depending on the number of children at the party, you can either have the guests take turns taking one valentine out of their bags at a time or have everyone open their valentines at once. Ask children to share their favorite valentines aloud with others. The loving words that are being shared will not only build friendship but nurture self-esteem.

Make It Memorable

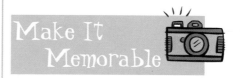

Give Valentine guests a little reminder of how much God loves them by preparing a "valentine from God" for each of them before the party begins. Write one thing God loves about each guest on a red construction paper heart. If you wish, you can add a Bible verse about God's love, as well. Sign each valentine "Love, God" or "Love, your heavenly Father."

Instructions:

- Have guests write their names on their lunch sacks and decorate with stickers, etc.

- Give every guest a set of hearts or valentines and have them write one to every person at the party—including themselves—saying one thing they like about that person.

- Set the lunch bags in a line and have guests put their valentines into the corresponding bags.

- Give each child a small bowl of prepared cake batter. Let them use food coloring to dye their batter the color of their choice.

- Put two cupcake papers in every cup of a muffin tin. Put a marble between the papers on one side. (This will make the cupcakes heart-shaped.)

- Fill each cup with individual batter, making sure children know which cupcake is theirs.

- Let guests open valentines while cupcakes bake and cool.

- Remove marbles from cupcake papers.

- Give children their specially dyed cupcakes and allow them to dip the tops in nondairy whipped topping, if they wish.

another
s i m p l e
Celebration

Easter Sunrise Celebration

May the glad dawn of Easter morn bring joy to thee.
—Easter Blessing

Easter is the oldest and most glorious celebration in the Christian tradition. While a visit by the Easter bunny is the norm, there are many more meaningful ways to help you and your family honor the sacred elements of the Easter season.

One such tradition is rising before daybreak to watch the sun rise on Easter Sunday morning. You can make this a small family gathering or invite friends, relatives, and extended family. You can watch from a nearby hill or the comfort of your own backyard. City dwellers may choose to watch from the roofs of their buildings. Once you've found a favorable location, this can become an annual event.

Word to the Wise: Easter is about new hope after tragedy. It is a time for the renewal of our hopes and dreams—even those we thought were dead.

Setting Up the Celebration:

- Find a suitable sunrise site. (You may even watch the sunrise from a window in your home or apartment.)

- Blanket or lawn chairs

- Breakfast foods (pop-up waffles, cinnamon toast, breakfast pastry, for example—whatever your family likes).

- Easy-to-read Bible translation

- Tree stems or twigs that exhibit buds, green leaves, signs of new growth. Easter branches are a centuries-old tradition in many countries. They represent resurrection, renewal, and new life.

Instructions:

- Once a meeting site has been chosen, contact those you want to invite with the time and date.

- When everyone has arrived, find your places—spread out the blanket, set up the chairs—or gather around the window.

- While waiting for the morning light to crest the horizon, one person should read from the Bible: Luke 24:1–6.

- Share a light breakfast together to celebrate this special event.

Easter Sunrise

The death and resurrection of Jesus Christ is the pivotal point of Christian faith—the foundation for teaching your children the reality of a relationship with God. Sure, your children will hear about the empty tomb in church, but you have a wonderful opportunity to really emphasize the gravity of the events that took place two thousand years ago. Why leave their understanding to chance? Get your family up early to worship the Risen Son.

Kids Can Too!

While breakfast is being prepared, send the children out to find Easter branches—small twigs or stems from trees or bushes with signs of new growth. (If you don't live where this is possible, you might gather a few the day before and let the children arrange them on the table.)

another simple Celebration

Easter Story Egg Hunt

A kiss at Christmas and an egg at Easter.
—Denham Tracts

Throughout the ages, eggs have been regarded as a symbol of life and rebirth. As early as the fourth century, people brought eggs to church to be blessed as a reminder of God's gift of new life. In the 1600s, eggs were dyed red during the Easter season. This color symbolized both joy and the blood shed on the cross.

Today, this tradition lives on as children prepare for Easter by dying eggs every color of the rainbow. You can carry on this tradition in a fresh new way by using the symbol of an egg to help teach the true story of Easter. By hunting for pieces of Scripture hidden in plastic eggs, your children can find something of lasting value this Easter season—a better understanding of Christ's sacrifice.

Word to the Wise: The truth behind the story of Easter is something worth searching for.

Setting Up the Celebration:

- Photocopy the Easter story from a copy of a large print or children's Bible. (Use Luke 24:1–8 for younger children and Matthew 27:62–28:10 for older children.)

- Carefully cut the photocopy into individual verses.

- Place each verse in a separate plastic egg.

- Fill as many other eggs as desired with small treats.

- Hide eggs in the house or outside, depending on the weather.

- If the children are under the age of four, invite parents to help their children search for the eggs.

- Make sure every child has a basket.

- Instruct children that no running is allowed.

- Come together as a group to open eggs.

- If the children are too young to read, place all of the pieces of Scripture together on a table and assist the children in putting the verses in order. If the children are older, have them read aloud any verses they have found, then try to put them together in order as a group.

- After the Easter story is complete, have one person read the finished Easter story aloud.

This Easter Story Egg Hunt can be used as a stand-alone activity for your own kids or a way to keep young guests occupied while you are putting the finishing touches on an Easter brunch for friends or relatives.

Moms on the Move

simple another be Celebration

$ Cost Savers

Easter can leave your family with an overabundance of hard-boiled eggs. Kids have fun dyeing them, hiding them, and finding them, but all too often they shy away from eating them. Don't waste money by letting these healthy Easter treats go to waste. Have your children help you remove the shells from the eggs they bring home. Cut the eggs in half and add 2 tbsp. mayonnaise, 1 tsp. vinegar, 1 tsp. prepared mustard, and ½ tsp. salt to every 12 egg yolk halves to make deviled eggs—or mash eggs together with the above ingredients to make egg salad sandwiches. (For egg salad, you may need to add a touch more mayo to suit your taste.)

Daddy's Day Breakfast in Bed

Father!—to God Himself we cannot give a holier name.
—William Wordsworth

Serving Dad breakfast in bed is one way to show him honor. It's also a way to help your children learn more about what it means to serve others. A Father's Day breakfast does not have to be an elaborate affair with fresh-squeezed orange juice and Eggs Benedict. It can be as simple as a cup of coffee and Disappearing Marshmallow Puffs. (See the recipe on the next page.) Young kids will have fun trying to figure out what made the marshmallows disappear, while you'll be amazed at how quickly these puffs disappear off Dad's plate!

Another simple idea for making the morning special is to serve Dad his coffee in a new Father's Day mug. If you plan ahead, you can order a mug with your children's photo on it. (These are usually available from photo studios at the mall or through various mail-order catalogs.)

While it's traditional to give gifts on Father's Day, remember that they are not the focus of the celebration—Dad is. Reminding him how much he is loved and appreciated throughout the year, not only on Father's Day, is a gift that only increases in value as the years go by.

Word to the Wise. Serving others in your family is one way of showing your love.

Setting Up the Celebration:

- Have kids draw pictures on Dad's breakfast napkins. (Supply Dad with an additional paper napkin so he doesn't have to destroy these works of art!)

- Have ingredients on hand for Disappearing Marshmallow Puffs:

  ¼ c. sugar, 2 cans refrigerated crescent rolls, ¼ c. melted butter, 1 tsp. cinnamon, and 16 large marshmallows

- Have a breakfast tray or TV table ready to serve Dad breakfast in bed.

Instructions:

- Let Dad sleep in while you set up the celebration.

- Once he wakes, you and the kids should greet Dad with hugs and kisses in bed, telling him to stay put!

- Give him the Sunday paper to enjoy while you're preparing his special breakfast.

- Help your kids prepare the Disappearing Marshmallow Puffs:

  Combine sugar and cinnamon. Dip marshmallows in melted butter (cooled a bit so children won't burn their fingers). Then, roll marshmallows in sugar mixture. Separate triangles of crescent rolls. Wrap each marshmallow in dough triangle, completely covering it and squeezing edges tight. Dip one side in melted butter and place it butter side down in a muffin tin. Place pan on a cookie sheet or foil. Bake at 375° for 10–15 minutes or until golden brown.

As you dress for the day, everyone except Dad gets to wear a red rose. (Use safety pins instead of straight pins to attach the rose to young children's clothing.) Wearing a single red rose in honor of your father (a white rose in honor of a father who has passed away) was the very first tradition established on the first Father's Day on June 19, 1910. Tell your children that if anyone asks them why they are wearing a rose, they should reply, "To celebrate my daddy!"

Kids Can Too!

Encourage your children to use their creativity to make a gift for Dad. Have them design their own card or write and perform an original song or poem. Have them create a personal gift from items they have on hand. For example, have them attach a photo on a paper plate and decorate the edges of the "frame" with artwork or stickers. Giving Dad a booklet of "I Love You" coupons makes a great gift. These homemade coupons could offer services such as a back rub, help mowing the lawn, an hour of quiet, making Dad laugh, or giving him a big hug and kiss.

another simple celebration

SIMPLE HOLIDAY CELEBRATIONS

Wet and Wild Independence Day Celebration

The United States of America themselves are essentially the greatest poem.
—Walt Whitman

When the July sun is burning bright on the Fourth, having a traditional Independence Day picnic or bar-be-que can be tough on kids and adults alike. But, that doesn't mean you have to retreat indoors. There are plenty of fun, easy, and inexpensive ways to make the day "cooler" in every sense of the word.

To make sure you are able to enjoy the party with everyone else, ask guests to bring one dish to share, their own meat to grill, and lawn chairs. You'll be able to invite more people, stay on budget, and spend more time personally enjoying a lazy day in the midst of a busy life.

Word to the Wise: Freedom is a gift from God worth celebrating.

Setting Up the Celebration:

- Invite friends by writing the party information in permanent marker on an uninflated beach ball.

- Encourage guests to bring swimsuits or wear clothes they won't mind getting wet. (Remind guests to bring a cover-up and plenty of sunscreen.)

- Pitch tents in the backyard.

- Have spray bottles filled with ice water sitting around for cooling yourself—or others. Freeze blueberries, maraschino cherries, or strawberries in ice cubes to cool drinks with a patriotic flair.

- Plan all of your activities around water—it's cheap, accessible, and the ultimate refreshment on a hot summer's day.

- At sunset, or before the main meal, gather together in prayer and thank God for those who gave their lives for this country. You may also want to spend time praising God for being the light of the world, living water, and offering your family the ultimate freedom of forgiveness.

Wet & Wild
Ways to Have Fun

- Give each child a squirt bottle filled with water or a clean paintbrush and a pail of water. Let kids paint water pictures on the sidewalk, deck, or fence.

- Fill a large tub with water. Add toys that float, plastic cups, a pitcher, sponges, a sieve, and a funnel. Just let the kids play! (Caution: A small child can drown in an amazingly small amount of water. Be absolutely sure someone is always watching.)

- Play catch—or volleyball—with water balloons.

- Try to knock over empty soda cans with the spray of a water pistol.

simple *another* *Celebration*

Good IDEA

Fireworks are an integral part of Independence Day celebrations. However, they can be dangerous, especially around children. Their use may also be illegal where you live. If you are not able to attend a public fireworks display, offer your kids some fun alternatives:

- Give kids new flashlights and have them make their own "fireworks" show in the sky after dark.

- Let kids cover themselves with glow-in-the-dark stickers. Then, let them play Hide-and-Seek in the backyard or basement.

- Buy birthday candles that don't blow out, but don't let your kids know. Place the lit candles on a Fourth of July cake and challenge your kids to extinguish them.

The Great Pumpkin Hunt

*I looked out my window and what did I find?
Green leaves a-growing on my pumpkin vine.*

—Author Unknown

From mid-October to mid-November, it's easy to find piles, rows, stacks, crates, boxes, even fields of pumpkins without searching too long. These orange wonders are inexpensive and have multiple uses. The best news is that children—and adults of all ages—find them charming.

In order to find the best selection, your family's Great Pumpkin Hunt should take place in late October or early November. Pumpkin farms are common across the country during those months. But even if you are limited to a few pumpkins stacked in front of the local supermarket, you can still have a great time and establish a yearly tradition for your family.

Inviting cousins, aunts and uncles, and grandparents, friends, and extended family makes the event even more fun. It also makes a great opportunity for a family picnic in the park, just when the leaves are changing and the weather is at its best.

Word to the Wise: Tell your children that pumpkins are like people—each one is unique in its own way.

Setting Up the Celebration:

- Scout out a suitable pumpkin search-and-purchase site.

- Draw a simple (really simple) map, placing a large X on the coordinates for the pumpkin site. Add time, date, place name, and your phone number. Make copies for your children to hand out to those they would like to invite to the hunt.

the Rules

- Upon arriving at the pumpkin location, each child is told to go in search of his or her "perfect pumpkin."

- If possible, assign one adult to each child.

- Let the children roam around the pumpkins, taking as much time as they like to make their selections. (Most children will change their minds often.)

- Each child should be allowed to purchase a pumpkin. But, stipulate that it must be one he or she can carry to the checkout.

- When selections have been made, write the name of each child on the top of the pumpkin near the stem.

If you're planning to make jack-o'-lanterns, a park is a great place to do it. Place newspapers on a picnic table, and let dads and grandpas do the cutting and emptying. Be sure to bring sturdy trash bags for the pumpkin guts. Place knives for carving the pumpkins in a shoe box rather than a paper bag for safety's sake. If you'd rather not get into carving, you can bring stickers and markers. Set the children around the picnic table and let them decorate to their hearts' content.

simple be another
celebration

MOM Meditations

Raising good-hearted, self-sufficient, well adjusted children is not dependent on how much money you are able to spend. The few dollars you shell out for a pumpkin can buy just as much fun for your child as a costly trip to a theme park or the newest designer toy—probably more. And it is a better opportunity to emphasize good values.

Don't get caught up in the hype or feel that you're failing your children because you choose in favor of simple fun. Just relax and enjoy yourself. That's the best thing you can do for yourself and your children.

SIMPLE HOLIDAY CELEBRATIONS

Thanksgiving Family Feast

Lord, help us to give Thee thanks for all we hold dear—
Not only on Thanksgiving Day but each day of the year!
—Author Unknown

The earliest recorded mention of a Thanksgiving celebration in Plymouth notes that four women and two teenaged girls prepared food for ninety Native American guests and fifty settlers. Hopefully, your guest list will be considerably smaller, and everyone in your family will lend a hand.

It's easy to let a Thanksgiving feast get out of hand when you try to include every dish associated with the holiday. Choose your menu carefully. Have every member of the family be in charge of one "specialty" dish. For younger children, that dish may be as simple as putting olives into a pretty dish. Older children may want to try their hand at homemade cranberry sauce or pumpkin-shaped cookies (a kid-friendly alternative to classic pumpkin pie).

Waiting for the turkey to cook can seem like forever to young children. Make the time go by more quickly, and enjoyably, by engaging your children and other young guests in a few simple holiday activities. They'll be thankful for the diversion, and so will you!

Festive Family Feast Activities

Let children prepare a Thanksgiving tablecloth runner. Cut a piece of butcher paper two feet longer than the length of your dining table or "kids" table. Invite the children to draw their own version of the first Thanksgiving.

Make Thanksgiving turkeys by having each child spread out his or her hand on a piece of colored paper. Draw a pencil outline around each individual finger. Let children add feet and color in the picture, using their thumb as the turkey's head and their fingers as its feathers.

Have kids write thank-you cards to God. Let them read their cards aloud after dinner is over.

Play "Stuff the Turkey!" Give each child a clean adult athletic sock (the "turkey"), a spoon, and a bowl of popped popcorn. The goal is for each child to stuff his or her "turkey" with spoonfuls of popcorn—holding the sock in one hand and the spoon in the other. After three minutes, the most "stuffed" sock wins!

Make your Thanksgiving feast a bit different by concluding your meal with prayer, rather than praying before you eat. But before you pray, go around the table and share one thing that you are especially thankful for this year. Once everyone has shared, you can open the time for anyone who wants to pray. You may even want to finish up with a simple song of thanks, such as "God Is So Good" or the doxology.

simple another Celebration

MOM Meditations

The busier you get, the easier it is to forget to say "thank you" to your kids, your spouse, and your Creator. Take a moment right now to quiet your heart. Think about the unique gifts that are wrapped up in each one of your children. Consider the things that first made you fall in love with your husband. Ponder how knowing God has made a difference in your life. Share your thoughts openly with God. Praise Him for His blessings. Ask Him to help you show your family how much you appreciate them, frequently and creatively.

Christmas Tree Treasures Celebration

The ornament of a house is the friends who frequent it.
—Ralph Waldo Emerson

There are many stories about how the Christmas tree became an important symbol of the holiday season. One often repeated tale is that Martin Luther was walking home one winter evening shortly before Christmas. As he looked at the stars shining through the branches of nearby evergreen trees, he was reminded of the everlasting life that Christ, the Light of the world, brought to earth through His birth. When Luther arrived home, he cut down a small evergreen tree. He placed candles on its branches, as a reminder of the stars—and Jesus' gift to the world.

Though strings of lights have long since replaced candles, the Christmas tree is still an important part of most families' holiday celebrations. You can turn a tradition into a memorable and meaningful celebration with a few simple additions to your usual tree-trimming time. While this can be a private, intimate family celebration, it is also a great time to invite friends—especially single parents or those who may be spending the season by themselves.

Word to the Wise: No matter how old you grow to be on this earth, you are "evergreen" in light of eternity, thanks to Jesus' gift of life.

Setting Up the Celebration:

- Cut down or purchase an evergreen tree. Trim a few inches off the trunk of the tree and let it sit in water for a few days before the celebration.

- If you wish, invite friends to join you on your chosen celebration date.

- Make or purchase a new ornament for every person at the celebration.

- Purchase a cross-shaped ornament for your family—or have an angel for the top of your tree.

- Make or purchase Christmas cookies or simple finger food, and apple cider.

- Untangle and test strings of lights, then place them on the tree.

- Put on a CD of Christmas carols.

- Put apple cider and a few cinnamon sticks in a Crock-Pot. Heat for about 45 minutes.

- To begin the celebration, take out your cross-shaped ornament or angel tree topper. Pray together as a family, thanking God for His eternal Christmas Gift.

- Have another child pass out the ornaments to each person. One at a time, open your ornaments and put them on the tree.

- Offer snacks and cider while you decorate the rest of the tree together.

simple another celebration

Make It Memorable

Your Christmas tree can be more than an attractive holiday decoration. It can become a treasure trove of memories. Be intentional in the ornaments you use. Along with the "First Christmas Together" and "Baby's First Christmas" ornaments that are often given as gifts, add ornaments representing events such as moving to a new home, taking up a new hobby, or enjoying a family vacation together. If the ornament you purchase is not dated, you can write the year in yourself with a fine-point permanent marker.

You can help your children begin their own future family tradition by helping them start their own ornament collection. Give each of them their own plastic storage bin to hold their growing collection. Every year, give them a new ornament when you put up the tree. You may also want to give them additional ornaments to represent significant family events such as vacations, the birth of a brother or sister, or awards they have won throughout the year. When the time comes for your children to move out on their own, they will already have the beginnings of a beautiful, and memorable, Christmas tradition.

Birthday Party for Jesus

*It is good to be children sometimes,
and never better than at Christmas,
when its mighty founder was a child Himself.*
—Charles Dickens

In all of the hustle and bustle of the Christmas season, it's easy to lose sight of the real reason for the celebration—the birth of Christ. Having a birthday party for Jesus first thing Christmas morning will help your family begin the day with the proper joyful focus. As you celebrate the eternal Gift you've received from God, it will keep the other temporal trinkets you receive during the day in a more balanced perspective.

The day you set up your Christmas tree, spend some time talking to your children about the true meaning of Christmas. As you tell them about God's Gift to the world, give them ideas about gifts they can give to God, such as breaking a bad habit, helping someone in need, worshipping God through song, or talking to Him in prayer. Ask them to think about what gift they would like to give to God this season.

When Christmas morning finally arrives, trade the old tradition of opening stockings filled with gifts from Santa for giving gifts of the heart to the Lord of the universe.

Word to the Wise: Jesus is the greatest gift anyone can ever receive.

Setting Up the Celebration:

- Several days before Christmas, help your children "wrap" their chosen gift to God. They may want to write out their gift of the heart in a card, draw it in a picture, or turn it into a song. Whatever they choose, help them create a tangible way to represent the gift, so it can be put under the tree with "For Jesus" written on it.

- Purchase a coffee cake or ingredients to make a simple breakfast "birthday" cake, such as "Jolly Jam Biscuits." (See recipe on following page.)

- Have birthday candles and matches on hand.

- Have a manger scene, without baby Jesus, set up in your home.

- Have an easy-to-understand version of the Christmas story available.

Good IDEA

As you give your gifts to Jesus on Christmas morning, talk about the other figures in the manger scene. Discuss how the gifts of praise given by the humble shepherds meant just as much to God as the expensive gifts given by the kings. Remind them that, at one time, Jesus was the same age as your children, so He knows what it feels like to go through the things they do.

Instructions:

- When children awaken, head downstairs as a family to prepare Jesus' birthday cake. Jolly Jam Biscuits are a quick and easy idea the whole family can help make: A jar of jam or preserves, 1 pkg. refrigerated biscuits, 2 tbsp. sugar, 1 egg, 2 tbsp. milk. Preheat the oven to 425°. Open can of biscuits, and arrange in a round pan so that they almost touch. Using clean fingers, press a tiny hollow in the center of each biscuit. Fill the hollow with a teaspoon of jam. Break egg into a bowl and beat until smooth. Beat in sugar and milk to make a glaze. Brush the glaze onto the biscuits. Bake about 10 minutes or until done. Cool in pan about 5 minutes.

- While breakfast is baking, read the Christmas story together.

- Place candles on coffee cake or Jolly Jam Biscuits.

- Set up manger scene, now with baby Jesus, on kitchen table.

- Sing "Happy Birthday, Dear Jesus" together as a family. Then, blow out candles.

- As a family, share your gifts to Jesus while you eat breakfast.

simple another celebration

JUST FOR THE FUN OF IT

JUST FOR THE FUN OF IT

Family Fun Bar-Be-Que

*It is not how much we have,
but how much we enjoy, that makes happiness.*
—Charles Spurgeon

You don't need a special occasion to make family mealtime more fun. A simple bar-be-que in the backyard makes any ordinary summer day feel like a party. It also gets you out of the kitchen when the temperature rises.

Easy preparation and cleanup make this an opportune time to let your kids invite their friends to join in on the fun. Treat the evening as a home-based camping trip. Play croquet on the lawn, but use potatoes instead of balls for unpredictable fun. Make s'mores over the coals. Tell tall family tales. And when the stars finally come out, see how many you can count.

You may even want to pitch a tent right there in your own backyard, bring out the sleeping bags, and bed down together for the night. When your schedule, or finances, are particularly tight, a minivacation like a back-yard bar-be-que can really help family morale.

Hot *Bar-be-que* Favorites

Make-Your-Own-Shish-Kebabs: Offer a variety of meats, fruits, and veggies, all cut into bite-sized pieces. Some tasty bar-be-que choices are shrimp, small cubes of beef, chicken, pork, turkey, hot dog, or sausage, cherry tomatoes, grapes, mushrooms, slices of zucchini, bell pepper, onion, banana, and pineapple. Let each person create his or her own personalized kabob, helping younger children safely "skewer" their choices. Offer sauces, such as sweet and sour, bar-be-que, teriyaki, or honey mustard, for dipping after the kabobs are done. Grill each kabob 10–20 minutes, or until the meat is fully cooked, turning frequently. Help young children remove their skewers.

Orange Bucket Cakes: Cut off the top quarter of an orange, saving it for later. Hollow out the inside of the orange. Fill about half full with prepared cake or muffin batter. Replace the top of the orange. Wrap the orange "bucket" tightly in foil. Bake it close to the coals for about 10 minutes or until the cake inside is done.

Hot Banana Split: Peel back one section of a banana. Spread with peanut butter. Add a few chocolate chips and miniature marshmallows. Replace the skin and wrap in foil. Grill for about 10 minutes, turning frequently.

Cool Side Dishes

- Pineapple Carrot Salad: Dissolve one small package of lemon-flavored gelatin in 1 c. boiling water. Stir one 13 ½-oz. can crushed pineapple, with juice from can, and 2 medium carrots, finely grated, into jello. Pour into a gelatin mold or serving bowl. Keep gel in refrigerator until set.

- Cupsicles: Fill small paper cups ¾ full with juice or pudding. Place cups in freezer. Once the contents become partially frozen but are still mushy, stick a plastic spoon into the middle of each cup, leaving the handle sticking up in the air. Freeze until solid. Let kids tear off paper cups and eat.

MOM Meditations

Any time you spend outdoors with your kids is a natural invitation to also spend time with God. When your kids are small, they may be the ones leading you in an impromptu worship service, by stopping to look at the wonder of a fallen leaf or the miracle of a fuzzy caterpillar. But, as your kids grow beyond the elementary school years, you can help them (and yourself) keep a childlike sense of wonder by taking time to really experience God's creation firsthand.

When God fills your heart with praise for all He has made, don't keep it to yourself. Tell your kids what you're feeling and how thankful you are. As a family, learn to stop, look, and listen when you're outside together. God's voice speaks clearly through all He has made.

JUST FOR THE FUN OF IT

Party on the Go

Traveling in the company with those we love is home in motion.

—Leigh Hunt

Road trips are a time-tested tradition for many families. Unfortunately, the longer the time on the road, the more everyone's patience seems to be tested. But that doesn't have to be the case. A car trip can actually be a celebration on the move, with a little bit of advance planning.

Carefully choose the route you will take. Review the pros and cons of different routes, contacting an automobile club for road construction information that may cause delays. If possible, take a different route home. The scenic route can be fun!

To break the possible monotony of a long trip, mix things up. Trade seats. Swap singing along with the radio with quiet times. Search for the funniest bumper sticker along the highway. Wear funny masks in the car (the driver should sit this game out) and watch the response from fellow travelers! At every rest stop, let one child use a highlighter on your road map to show how far you've traveled since the last stop. The more creative you are, the more fun you'll have.

Setting Up
the Celebration:

- Before leaving, spend some time on the Internet checking out the larger towns you'll be driving through along the way. Scheduling brief stops at minidestinations along the road, such as an offbeat museum or a city park, can make travel days more fun.

- Let each child take one backpack of "on the road" diversions. If it doesn't fit in the backpack, it has to stay at home!

- Wrap several inexpensive "surprises" to be opened during the trip by each child. Funky sunglasses, favorite snacks, a CD the family can enjoy, or a small toy all work well.

- Bring bubbles, a ball, jump rope, etc., to be used at rest stops. A ten-minute playtime can burn off a little pent-up energy for both you and the kids.

- While on the road, schedule a half hour of quiet time twice a day. This is the time to look out the window and talk to God.

- Give each child a disposable camera at the beginning of the trip. When you return, help your kids make individual "memory" albums with their pictures or put everyone's photos together for a fun family keepsake.

Your own attitude can make a big difference on a car trip. If you're dreading a long drive, your kids may end up feeling the same way. Treat every road trip as an adventure. Ask God to help you enjoy the scenery along the way, as well as the opportunity to talk with your kids about nothing and everything. Turn off the radio or CD player now and then. Ask your kids questions about what they like best about their lives, what they think about God, and what they'd like to do when they grow up.

simple another Celebration

Cost Savers

Eating out along the road can really add up, especially when you have kids who want a soda with every meal or snacks at every gas station. Save money, and stress, by planning ahead. Let kids pick out a few healthy snacks at the grocery store before you leave. Make your own "Zoo Food Gorp" by mixing 2 c. animal crackers, 1 c. salted peanuts, ½ c. raisins, and ½ c. candy-coated chocolate candies into individual bags. Give each child his or her own water bottle to keep in the cooler. Or, you can give each child a travel expense budget to spend on snacks or souvenirs. This can help them learn how to budget their money.

Super BOWL Party

*When a man's stomach is full
it makes no difference whether he is rich or poor.*
—Euripides

You don't have to enjoy football to enjoy a Super BOWL party. The most successful celebrations cater to diehard fans as well as those who'd rather just sit around and "chew the fat" while they're munching the chips.

To make sure that your celebration meets the expectations of both of these groups, ask your guests beforehand which group they feel they fit more closely into. This way, you can be prepared for those who want to concentrate on the game, while making a comfortable spot farther away from the television (perhaps even in another room!) for those who could really care less about the outcome.

With a few simple preparations, and some super bowls of food, you can score a memorable day for yourself and your guests, regardless of what happens on the field.

Setting Up the Celebration:

- When you invite your guests, ask them to wear their favorite team's colors and bring one "super" bowl of food.

- Set up adequate seating near the television that is both viewer- and food-friendly. Have a comfortable area at the kitchen or dining room table for those guests who'd rather sit and chat.

- Provide paper and crayons to any children who attend, and ask them to draw footballs to decorate the buffet area.

- You may want to have a video in another room, if possible, to keep younger children occupied during the game. Or, if a few of the moms aren't interested in the game on TV, they could help organize a kid-friendly football tournament in the basement or backyard.

- Place each bowl of munchies on the kitchen counter, along with disposable plates, cups, and silverware. Have guests prepare their own plates before finding their seats for the game.

Super BOWL
Recipe Ideas

Kids Can Too!

Touchdown Chicken Wings: Mix ⅔ c. soy sauce and 2 c. packed light brown sugar in a medium mixing bowl. Arrange 24 chicken wings or drummettes, skin removed, in a greased 9×13-inch baking dish. Pour sauce over chicken. Bake at 300° for 3 hours. Serve in large bowl.

Cheerleader Chow: Melt ½ c. butter (one stick). Stir in 1 c. peanut butter. Stir in one box Crispix cereal (12.3 oz.) and 12 oz. chocolate chips. After cereal is coated, stir in 1 lb. powdered sugar. After cooled, serve in super bowl.

Even if your kids are too young to enjoy watching the game, they can still play a special part in a Super BOWL celebration. Give them the task of coming up with their own halftime show. Let them choose one or two songs from their favorite CD. Then, have them prepare to lip sync a song and dance routine during the first half of the game. During halftime, have the adults take time out from the televised show to watch their own tiny stars perform.

simp*another* celebration

Kids' Slumber Party

*There never was a child so lovely
but his mother was glad to get him asleep.*
—Ralph Waldo Emerson

In a kid's world, staying up past bedtime is a party in itself. Inviting friends over to share this experience makes it even more memorable. Slumber parties shouldn't be reserved for birthdays. Since most kids just enjoy hanging out together and doing "nothing," you don't need to do a lot of physical preparation.

However, being mentally prepared for the evening is another topic altogether. That's because a kid's dream-come-true can easily turn into a parent's nightmare. Having one of your children's friends spend the night is usually easy to handle. Having half a dozen pajama-clad kids racing through your house can easily put you out of the partying mood.

Begin by preparing yourself mentally for a late night. Try to remember what it's like to be your kid's age. Take what you remember and act on it. Make sure there's a nightlight in the room the kids will be sleeping in, as well as the closest bathroom. Be patient with late-night snickers. Have compassion for kids who wake up grumpy after a late night. And enjoy your kids enjoying themselves.

Activities
to Tucker Out
Tiny Guests

Ask each guest to bring an extra-large, white adult T-shirt with them to the party. Cover your kitchen table or floor with newspaper. Have one large piece of cardboard for each guest and an assortment of permanent markers or puffy pen paints. Invite guests to decorate their shirts with their own original design. Do this early in the party so the shirts have time to dry before bedtime. At bedtime, have the guests put on their new nightshirts. Let them know that they can wear their shirts over their own pajamas, if they prefer.

Have the children lie on the floor in a circle, each one with her head on another guest's stomach. Have each child give a hearty fake laugh. Soon, everyone will be giggling without faking it.

Have a mini pillow fight by giving each guest a pair of socks rolled into a ball. The rules are that you can only have one pair of socks at a time. This keeps kids scrambling and dodging without hurting themselves as they might with pillows.

When it's time for "lights out" (the exact time of which you and your child should agree on before the party even begins), you can expect a few giggles to continue for awhile afterward. You may want to give your guests a half hour warning before bedtime arrives, to help prepare them for the inevitable. It's a good idea to let kids enjoy any rowdy activities you have planned earlier in the evening, saving quieter activities for later on. A good way to help kids wind down is to have them climb into their sleeping bags to watch a video. If the kids are still having trouble quieting down later on, remind them that you can grab a sleeping bag and join them. That usually quiets them right down!

Good IDEA

When you're having a group of kids spend the night, it's a good idea to keep the snacks fairly low in sugar and easy to get out of the carpet. Providing individual bottles of juice or sports drinks, particularly those with squirt-bottle lids, is a better choice than easily tipped over cans of soda. Popcorn or gummy snacks are popular treats that are also hassle free. Stay away from anything that melts, stains, or contains caffeine.

simple *another* Celebration

Dark and Stormy Night

The dog was whimpering beside the bed again. "Some watchdog," Jessie muttered under her breath. "Afraid of a little thunder." With a yawn and a sigh, Jessie closed her eyes only to jerk them wide open again as a clap of thunder shook the windows. A parade of hurried footsteps immediately followed.

"Can we climb in?" her five-year-old son, Connor, asked with a shudder.

"Pleeeeease!" pleaded his three-year-old sister, Jamie, seemingly close to tears.

Jessie pulled up the covers like a makeshift tent and invited the two inside. By then, Matt was stirring beside her. Thunder, ringing phones, and insistent alarm clocks usually had little effect on her husband. But tonight, the lightning seemed to be making a direct hit on the Clarkson home.

The children shivered and whispered as they snuggled together under the blankets. As Jessie held them close, she recalled another storm years before. This time Jessie was the frightened little girl hopping in bed with her parents. As her father's snores competed with the cracks of thunder, Jessie's mom had invited her to a special party that night—a Lightning Party.

Jessie's mom put a blanket over the railings at the top of the landing, forming a cozy hideaway from which they could look out the big picture window at God's fireworks display. Beneath the blanket, they fashioned a nest of old quilts and feather pillows. Huddled together, nestled snug in their fortress against the storm, they sipped hot chocolate and counted the seconds between each flash of light and its corresponding crash of thunder.

Jessie and her mom chatted about nothing and everything—the different sounds that God could have chosen to give thunder, the bully in Jessie's music class, whether hot chocolate was better topped with marshmallows or whipped cream, and where cats hide when it rains. All too soon, the thunder had faded away, but that night began a tradition that lasted well into Jessie's teenage years. Thunder after bedtime had always been an invitation for a mother-and-daughter celebration.

Some traditions are too important to be forgotten, Jessie thought.

"Time for a party!" Jessie whispered to Jamie and Connor, who giggled with a mixture of delight and disbelief. Together they gathered blankets, pillows, and the still-whimpering dog and cuddled together on the living-room floor. As they looked out the front window and sipped hot cocoa, they talked about nothing and everything—why some thunder cracked and some rumbled, what marshmallows were made of, why Carly next door could use a friend, and how a little girl named Jessie, once afraid of thunder, grew to anticipate its arrival like an unexpected holiday.

the end

JUST FOR THE FUN OF IT

Movie Night Pizza Party

The most useless day is that on which we have not laughed.

—Charles Field

With the convenience of videos, DVDs, and HBO, having a movie night together as a family, or with a group of friends, is a common pastime. You can turn it into a minicelebration with a few quick changes. First, make your seating area as cozy as possible. If you're watching a movie with the kids, you may even want to set up a family "fort" from which to watch the film. Add atmosphere to your "theatre" by lighting the room solely with candles.

Also, while ordering a pizza is something of a movie-at-home tradition, it can be less expensive and more fun to make your own together. If you like, you can begin the film as it bakes, then break for a pizza intermission. This inter-mission can be a good time to "switch seats." This will prevent one person from dominating the "choice" seat throughout the entire evening.

A simple party game can add a festive feel to the evening. Put a sticker on the bottom of one of the dinner plates. Whoever gets this plate either gets a free video rental coupon or can pick the next film the family rents together.

Movie
Night Calzone:

You will need one loaf of thawed bread dough plus toppings of your choice. Some ideas:

Spinach Topping: One egg white, 6 oz. center cut bacon (chopped), ½ c. chopped onion, one 10-oz. pkg. chopped frozen spinach (thawed and strained), ¼ tsp. garlic salt, 1 c. shredded Monterey Jack cheese. In a medium skillet, cook bacon. Drain. Add spinach, onion, and garlic salt, and cook several minutes. Stir in cheese and mix well.

Sausage Topping: 1 lb. Italian sausage, 1 c. shredded provolone cheese, 1 c. shredded mozzarella cheese, ¼ c. grated Parmesan cheese. In a medium skillet, cook sausage. Drain. Stir in cheese and mix well.

Antipasto Topping: 6 oz. each: sliced capicola ham, hard salami, pepperoni, sliced provolone cheese, sliced mozzarella cheese. Layer each down center of dough. Optional: Top with sliced black olives.

Roll out bread dough on floured countertop to ½-inch thick. Spread desired filling down center of dough. Bring long sides of loaf together, covering filling. Seal sides and tuck the ends under. Place on a greased cookie sheet, with seam side down. Brush with egg white. Bake at 350° for 30–40 minutes or until golden brown. Cool 7–10 minutes and cut into ¾-inch slices. Serves 10–12.

Dessert Pizza

You'll need one can refrigerated crescent rolls, 8 oz. softened cream cheese, $1/3$ c. sugar, assorted fruits, such as kiwi, strawberries, blueberries, seedless grapes, or mandarin oranges. Lightly spray a pizza pan with nonstick cooking spray. Spread the crescent roll dough on pan, pinching seams together. Bake 10–15 minutes at 350° or until golden brown. Let cool completely. Combine cream cheese and sugar until blended. Spread over cooled crust. Arrange fruit on cream cheese. Chill. Cut into wedges and serve. Serves 8–10.

simple another
be celebration

Good IDEA

After the credits roll, save some time for conversation. Even if the kids have to head off to bed, talk about the movie with your spouse. Since every movie is a story, it has the potential to teach a lesson. What lesson was this movie trying to teach? Is the message one you agree with? How would you have told the story differently? What would God have to say about what you just saw? When you get the chance, talk to your kids about what they saw and discuss some of the same questions.

Pamper Yourself Party

*Just as lotions and fragrance give sensual delight,
a sweet friendship refreshes the soul.*
—Proverbs 27:9, THE MESSAGE

Every busy mom needs a break now and then. Inviting other women over for an evening of rest and relaxation may take some organization, but the benefits are worth it.

The only two things this party requires are hardworking moms like yourself and a dependable baby-sitter. This is one party where no kids are allowed! Ask women to encourage their spouses to have a "night out" with the kids. Once these two things are taken care of, the rest of the evening's activities—or lack thereof—are up to you. Think about all of the things you'd like to do. Then, figure out how to offer these options to your friends, as well as yourself.

If the activities you offer cost more money than you can afford, don't be afraid to let your guests know beforehand that a donation of five dollars, or whatever you feel is reasonable, is appreciated. Don't forget to enjoy the evening along with your guests. Save clean-up for tomorrow. Tonight, relax and enjoy the company.

Pampering Pleasures

Ask each guest to bring something chocolate to set out for a dessert buffet.

Invite women to come in their pajamas or sweats and forego any makeup.

Hire a masseuse for the evening. Let her know what you're planning, and see if she is willing to work for just tips and the "kitty" donation. Let interested guests schedule a 15-minute "appointment," reminding them that tips are appreciated.

Ask guests to bring any jewelry or clothing they no longer wear for a fashion exchange. Put everything on a table and let guests take what they need.

Have a quiet corner by a fireplace, or accented by lit candles, where women can just sit and relax.

If you have access to a hot tub, encourage women to bring their suits and enjoy.

Have a table set up with nail polish, nail polish remover, nail files, and manicure scissors. Invite women to give themselves, or each other, a manicure or pedicure.

As the evening begins to wind down, have a "chick flick" on DVD ready for any women who are able to stay later than the others.

After relaxing at a "Pamper Yourself" party, you and your guests may decide that you've enjoyed it so much that you'd like to make it a regular tradition. Trade host houses and switch activities. Be sure to invite new friends. This is one party that works as well with five as it does with twenty-five.

simple *another* celebration

MOM *Meditations*

Taking time out for yourself is an important part of being a good mom to your kids. It helps you lead, and model, a more balanced life. Especially when your kids are small and their demands on your time seem to be constant, even a small break can make a big difference. Take advantage of any time you have before the kids get up in the morning, while they nap, or when they're in their rooms for some "quiet time" of their own. The chores will still be there once you're done.

Take a long bubble bath while reading a good book—one that's not on parenting. Sit down with a cup of tea and one really great cookie, and listen to a favorite CD while just looking out the window. Turn on a worship CD, lie down on the couch, close your eyes, and talk to your heavenly Father.

Teddy Bear Tea Party

You can discover more about a person in an hour of play than in a year of conversation.
—Plato

Little girls, and big ones, too, love a tea party. Although most tea parties are reserved for girls, boys under the age of six may enjoy dressing up in their dads' suits and ties for the special occasion, as well. And a tea party should be a special occasion! That doesn't mean that you have to slave all night setting up a fancy table and baking special treats. A kids' tea party is more about pretend than it is about protocol.

Invite your guests to come all dressed up in their parents' clothes. Little girls can also be asked to bring along a favorite doll or teddy bear dressed for the occasion. Your role is to play the "humble servant." Greet every child at the door with a "Welcome, Miss" or "Good afternoon, Sir." Treating kids like grown-ups will get them in the "let's pretend" mood the moment they enter the door.

Setting Up
the Celebration:

- Set up a table with enough chairs for your young guests. If there is enough room at the table, supply a chair for each teddy bear, as well.

- Cover the table with a disposable or washable tablecloth. Set the table with kid-sized plastic or paper plates. If a child's plastic tea set is available, use the cups for your guests. If not, any plastic cup will do. If your tea party will be in a carpeted area, place a plastic tablecloth beneath your table.

- Decorate the table with a small bouquet of flowers or a pretty doll as a centerpiece. You can also fill an empty toilet roll with tiny surprises, wrap in tin foil, and twist the ends to make English "party cracker" favors.

- Have apple juice (a kid's version of "tea") and a few treats on hand. Peanut butter or grilled cheese sandwiches cut with cookie cutters work well. A box of fancy-shaped butter cookies completes the menu.

- Have a camera and film ready. If you have a video camera, you may want to use it.

- Make "ribbons" for the winners of the costume contest.

Instructions:

- Greet the guests "formally" at the door.

- Have a guest and teddy bear parade around the house with music. Invite other moms to stay until the parade has finished.

- Take photos of each child holding her bear.

- Serve "tea" from a fancy teapot, accompanied by snacks.

- Have a costume contest making sure each child wins a small prize. Categories could include: Most Original, Best Dressed, Most Grown-Up, Best Mom and Bear Outfits.

simp b another celebration

Make It Memorable

The photos you take during a dress-up party are ones that will be treasured for years to come. Instead of just putting them into a photo album, you can make them more "visible" by transferring the photos onto mugs that can be given to the children at Christmastime or for a birthday. Let the kids' moms know what you'd like to do and see if they are interested in purchasing a gift like this for their children. You may be able to get a discount at a photo lab for multiple orders.

Children will enjoy drinking out of their dress-up cup on special occasions. Just be forewarned: They may ask you to address them as "miss" or "sir"!

JUST FOR THE FUN OF IT

Getting to Know You Brunch

The love we give away is the only love we keep.
—Elbert Hubbard

Making a new friend is like opening a treasure chest: You never know what priceless gems you'll find inside. Yet for busy moms, it's often easier to rely on the companionship of old friends than to take time to nurture new ones. Why miss out on what could become a lifelong blessing? A brunch is a great way to make a newcomer feel at home, while opening your own heart to the possibility of friendship.

Whether the woman you want to invite is new to your neighborhood, church, or work, or someone you've known casually for years, find a time that is convenient for her. Then, invite a few members of your regular "gang" to help keep the conversation going. Let them know that the focus of the brunch is not just fun, but to make the guest of honor feel comfortable.

What do you have to lose? All you need is a few free hours, quick and tasty recipes, a handful of old friends, and one or two new acquaintances. Mix them together with love—and enjoy!

Word to the Wise: Love longs to make others feel at home.

Easy, Yet *Elegant* Brunch *Ideas*

Crescent Chicken Puffs: ½ c. seasoned croutons (crushed), ¼ c. pecans (chopped fine), 3 oz. cream cheese, 2 tbsp. butter (softened), ¾ tsp. lemon pepper, 1 ¼ c. cooked chicken (diced), 1 small can mushrooms (drained and chopped), 1 can refrigerated crescent rolls, and ¼ c. butter (melted). Mix the croutons and pecans on a plate. In a bowl, mix the cream cheese, butter, lemon pepper, chicken, and mushrooms. Separate the crescent rolls. Place two heaping teaspoons of chicken mixture on each triangular roll. Roll up like regular crescent rolls, but tuck the sides and point under. Press the edges together to seal. Dip rolls in melted butter, then roll in crouton mixture. Bake in shallow pan at 375° for 15 minutes or until golden brown. Serves 8.

Raspberry Spinach Salad: 2 tbsp. raspberry vinegar, 2 tbsp. raspberry jam, ⅓ c. vegetable oil, 8 c. spinach (rinsed, stemmed, and torn), ¾ c. chopped macadamia nuts, 1 c. fresh raspberries, 3 sliced kiwis. Combine vinegar and jam in blender or small bowl. Add a thin stream of oil, blending well. Toss spinach with half the nuts, half the raspberries, and half the kiwis and dressing in a salad bowl. Top with remaining nuts, raspberries, and kiwis. Serves 8.

Chocolate Chip Cream Cheese Brownies: (Prepare this the night before.) 1 pkg. refrigerated chocolate chip cookie dough, 8 oz. softened cream cheese, 1 egg, ½ c. sugar, and ½ tsp. vanilla. Lightly coat an 8×8-square baking pan with nonstick cooking spray. Take half the cookie dough and press into bottom of prepared pan. Combine the cream cheese, egg, sugar, and vanilla. Spread over the pressed cookie dough. Roll the remaining dough out fairly thin. Place it on top of the cream cheese layer, covering it as thoroughly as possible. Bake for 30–35 minutes in a 350° oven or until cream cheese sets. Let stand. Cool in fridge overnight. Slice into squares. Makes 9–12 servings.

simple another Celebration

As you prepare for the brunch, remember that the focus is friendship, not your homemaking skills. Relax. Be intentional in your conversation. Be sensitive to when your guest wants to speak and when she doesn't. And really listen to her answers.

Kids Can Too!

As you practice making others feel at home, your kids will see hospitality in action. This will help teach them how easy, and important, it is to risk making new friends. When a new kid joins their class at school, or moves in around the corner, encourage your kids to have a "getting to know you" party of their own. You make the food and let your kids supply the friendship.

Come in the evening, come in the morning,

Come when expected, come without warning,

Thousands of welcomes you'll find here before you,

And the oftener you come, the more we'll adore you.

—Irish Saying